Informing the legislative debate since 1914 _____

The Fourth Amendment Third-Party Doctrine

Richard M. Thompson II
Legislative Attorney

June 5, 2014

Congressional Research Service

7-5700

www.crs.gov

R43586

Summary

In the 1970s, the Supreme Court handed down *Smith v. Maryland* and *United States v. Miller*, two of the most important Fourth Amendment decisions of the 20th century. In these cases, the Court held that people are not entitled to an expectation of privacy in information they voluntarily provide to third parties. This legal proposition, known as the third-party doctrine, permits the government access to, as a matter of Fourth Amendment law, a vast amount of information about individuals, such as the websites they visit; who they have emailed; the phone numbers they dial; and their utility, banking, and education records, just to name a few. Questions have been raised whether this doctrine is still viable in light of the major technological and social changes over the past several decades.

Before there were emails, instant messaging, and other forms of electronic communication, it was much easier for the courts to determine if a government investigation constituted a Fourth Amendment "search." If the police intruded on your person, house, papers, or effects—tangible property interests listed in the text of the Fourth Amendment—that act was considered a search, which had to be "reasonable" under the circumstances. However, with the advent of intangible forms of communication, like the telephone or the Internet, it became much more difficult for judges to determine when certain surveillance practices intruded upon Fourth Amendment rights. With *Katz v. United States*, the Court supposedly remedied this by declaring that the Fourth Amendment protects not only a person's tangible things, but additionally, his right to privacy. *Katz*, however, left unprotected anything a person knowingly exposes to the public. This idea would form the basis of *Smith* and *Miller*. In those cases, the Court held that a customer has no reasonable expectation of privacy in the phone numbers he dials (*Smith*) and in checks and deposit slips he gives to his bank (*Miller*), as he has exposed them to another and assumed the risk they could be handed over to the government.

While the third-party doctrine has been criticized by Members of Congress, various commentators, and others as overly constrictive of Americans' privacy rights, it appears to fit relatively well with other Fourth Amendment case law. That being said, advancements in data collection, automation, and use have some questioning the continued application of this doctrine in a digital society. Several events have precipitated renewed debates over its continued existence. First was the Supreme Court's decision in the GPS tracking case, *United States v. Jones*, where two concurring opinions comprising five Justices of the Court called into question various existing Fourth Amendment theories, including the third-party doctrine, at least with respect to long-term government monitoring and advanced surveillance technology. Second was the Edward Snowden leaks relating to the National Security Agency's telephone metadata program, which has been primarily justified by *Smith* and the third-party doctrine. Various Members of Congress have joined the debate, with some introducing legislation that would require a warrant for access to records held by third-parties, and others introducing more targeted measures that would limit access to information such as geolocation data from third-party companies.

With these legal, social, and technological trends in mind, this report explores the third party-doctrine, including its historical background, its legal and practical underpinnings, and its present and potential future applications. It explores the major third-party doctrine cases and fits them within the larger Fourth Amendment framework. It surveys the various doctrinal and practical arguments for and against its continued application. Lastly, this report describes congressional efforts to supplement legal protection for access to third-party records, as well as suggesting possible future directions in the law.

Contents

Contacts

Introduction

In 1967, the Supreme Court pronounced in *Katz v. United States* that "[w]hat a person knowingly exposes to the public, even in his own home or office, is not a subject of Fourth Amendment protection."[1] This rule "that a person has no legitimate expectation of privacy in information he voluntarily turns over to third parties" is known as the "third-party doctrine."[2] While its reach in the pre-digital age was relatively limited, the third-party doctrine has provided the government a powerful investigative tool in a society where people share ever-increasing amounts of information with others. Many have debated whether these technological and social changes require the courts to reconsider this doctrine, or, alternatively, whether Congress should step in and create some form of statutory protection for this information.[3]

Over the years, the Court has applied the third-party doctrine to two main sets of cases. In one, the Court has held that people do not have a reasonable expectation that a person with whom they are communicating will not later reveal that conversation to the police.[4] In the second, the Court extended this doctrine to hold that people are not entitled to Fourth Amendment safeguards for records given to a third-party or data generated as part of a person's business transactions with a third-party. In two of the most prominent third-party cases, *Smith v. Maryland* and *United States v. Miller*, the Court held that government access to telephone calling records and bank records, respectively, were not Fourth Amendment searches for which warrants were required.[5]

To be clear, the third-party doctrine does not cover all conceivable information that is transferred through a third party. For instance, the content of a voice or email communication does not fall within its scope.[6] The courts have reasoned that the service provider is merely the conduit or intermediary of those communications and not the recipient; thus, the user does not lose privacy protection in those communications. On the other hand, both non-content and content information that is shared directly with a service provider is covered by the third-party doctrine (e.g., the deposit slips or checks shared with a bank and data kept by the bank relating to transactions with it). Additionally, non-content information derived from private interactions with others is subject to the third-party doctrine. This covers data such as telephone numbers dialed, email addresses of those emailed, or websites visited.

---

[1] Katz v. United States, 389 U.S. 347, 351 (1967).

[2] Smith v. Maryland, 442 U.S. 735, 743-44 (1979).

[3] *See, e.g.,* Orin Kerr and Greg Nojeim, *The Data Question: Should the Third-Party Records Doctrine Be Revisited?*, ABA JOURNAL (Aug. 1, 2012), *available at* http://www.abajournal.com/magazine/article/ the_data_question_should_the_third-party_records_doctrine_be_revisited/; Orin Kerr, *The Case for the Third Party Doctrine*, 107 MICH. L. REV. 561, 575 (2009); Richard A. Epstein, *Privacy and the Third Hand: Lessons from the Common Law of Reasonable Expectations*, 24 BERKELEY TECH. L. J. 1199 (2009); Erin Murphy, *The Case Against the Case for Third-Party Doctrine: A Response to Epstein and Kerr*, 24 BERKELEY TECH. L. J. 1239 (2009); Stewart Baker, Smith v. Maryland *as a Good First-Order Estimate of Reasonable Privacy Expectations*, VOLOKH CONSPIRACY (May 4, 2014), *available at* http://www.washingtonpost.com/news/volokh-conspiracy/wp/2014/05/04/smith-v-maryland-as-a-good-first-order-estimate-of-reasonable-privacy-expectations/.

[4] *See infra* notes 49-66, and accompanying cases.

[5] United States v. Miller, 425 U.S. 435 (1976); *Smith*, 442 U.S. 735.

[6] *Katz*, 389 U.S. at 352 (voice); United States v. Warshak, 631 F.3d 266, 288 (6th Cir. 2010) (email).

The third-party doctrine has been heavily criticized for unnecessarily constricting Americans' privacy rights.[7] But whatever one thinks of the rule that citizens are not entitled to Fourth Amendment protection when they share information with one another, the third-party doctrine is largely entrenched in other areas of Fourth Amendment case law. For example, it is not a Fourth Amendment search for the police to dig through one's trash left on the curb,[8] to track a person's movements on public streets,[9] and even to surveil a person in a fenced-in backyard with an aircraft.[10] In each of these instances, the Court reasoned that because the person exposed his activities to the public gaze he was no longer entitled to an expectation of privacy.

In addition to the legal attacks on the third-party doctrine, some have questioned its practical implications in a society which shares almost every facet of its life with various entities.[11] Both *Smith* and *Miller*, decided in the mid- to late-1970s, came before the mass digital revolution experienced over the last several decades. Since these decisions, there has been a wave of advancement in data generation, collection, automation, and processing.[12] Whether these new technologies and shifts in social interaction require courts or lawmakers to revise this review is currently under debate.

Two major events in the past few years typify this ongoing debate. The first is the conversation prompted by several concurrences in the 2012 GPS tracking case *United States v. Jones*.[13] In two concurring opinions in that case, five Justices opined that warrantless, pervasive government location monitoring can violate the Fourth Amendment.[14] Commentators have speculated that these five votes could have significant consequences for other similar ubiquitous surveillance techniques.[15] And at least one member of the Court, Justice Sotomayor, believes that the third-

---

[7] *See, e.g.*, United States v. Miller, 425 U.S. 435, 447 (Brennan, J., dissenting); Stephen E. Henderson, *The Timely Demise of the Fourth Amendment Third Party Doctrine*, 96 Iowa L. Rev. Bull. 396 (2011); Christopher Slobogin, Privacy at Risk: The New Government Surveillance and the Fourth Amendment 140 (2007).

[8] California v. Greenwood, 486 U.S. 35, 43-44 (1988).

[9] United States v. Knotts, 460 U.S. 276, 285 (1983).

[10] Florida v. Riley, 488 U.S. 445, 451-52 (1989).

[11] *See* Daniel J. Solove, The Digital Person: Technology and Privacy in the Information Age 202 (2004) ("The government's harvesting of information from the extensive dossiers being assembled with modern computer technology poses one of the most significant threats to privacy of our time.").

[12] Omer Tene and Jules Polonetsky, *Big Data for All: Privacy and User Controls in the Age of Analytics*, 11 Nw. J. Tech. & Intell. Prop. 239, *1(2013) ("Big data is upon us." https://a next.westlaw.com/Document/ I535f4a8bb78611e28578f7ccc38dcbee/View/FullText html?navigationPath= Search%2Fv3%2Fsearch%2Fresults%2Fnavigation%2Fi0ad6040300000146014bbf3f6cbb1298%3FNav%3DANALY TICAL%26fragmentIdentifier%3DI535f4a8bb78611e28578f7ccc38dcbee%26startIndex%3D1%26contextData%3D% 2528sc.Search%2529%26transitionType%3DSearchItem&listSource=Search&listPageSource= 4f65f444bd87ab8451abbca5a750d542&list=ANALYTICAL&rank=10&grading=na&sessionScopeId= bbd4e55d34300e25e857bc0ccd7bbb05&originationContext=Search%20Result&transitionType=SearchItem& contextData=%28sc.Search%29 - co_footnote_F3388167494 Over the past few years, the volume of data collected and stored by business and government organizations has exploded. The trend is driven by reduced costs of storing information and moving it around in conjunction with increased capacity to instantly analyze heaps of unstructured data using modern experimental methods, observational and longitudinal studies, and large scale simulations. Data are generated from online transactions, email, video, images, clickstream, logs, search queries, health records, and social networking interactions; gleaned from increasingly pervasive sensors deployed in infrastructure such as communications networks, electric grids, global positioning satellites, roads and bridges, as well as in homes, clothing, and mobile phones.").

[13] United States v. Jones, 132 S. Ct. 945 (2012).

[14] *Id.* at 954 (Sotomayor, J., concurring); *Id.* at 957 (Alito, J., concurring).

[15] *See, e.g.*, Priscilla J. Smith, *Much Ado About Mosaics: How Original Principles Apply to Evolving Technology in* (continued...)

party doctrine should be seriously rethought as a whole. The second is the litigation surrounding the National Security Agency's telephone metadata program. Several federal courts, including the Foreign Intelligence Surveillance Court, have applied *Smith* and the third-party doctrine to uphold this comprehensive data collection program.[16] One district court judge, however, found *Smith* outdated and the NSA program too invasive for *Smith* to still control this legal question.[17]

With these shifts in technology and legal thinking in mind, this report explores the history and legal foundations of the third-party doctrine. It will first provide background to the Fourth Amendment and describe in what instances government investigations trigger its protections. It will then analyze the Court's third-party doctrine cases and provide doctrinal and practical arguments for and against its application. Next, this report will examine how Congress has responded to the third-party doctrine and whether *United States v. Jones* and subsequent cases might alter its future application. Lastly, this report will consider any potential future developments in this fast-moving area of law.

Fourth Amendment Background

Before the advent of modern communications, government officials could not simply subpoena an Internet Service Provider (ISP), or Amazon, or Google for information relating to a target of investigation, but had to enter the suspect's home or office, sometimes by force, to retrieve personal information directly themselves.[18] During the 18th century, British and colonial officials conducted searches and seizures of people's homes with little to no suspicion of wrongdoing pursuant to either a general warrant, which was used mainly in England, or a writ of assistance, which was used in the American colonies.[19] These indiscriminate government intrusions contributed to the people's fear of unrestrained government power and led to the eventual passage of the Fourth Amendment.

Take, for instance, the formative English search and seizure case *Entick v. Carrington*, where the government was investigating John Entick and others for alleged publication of seditious articles.[20] In that case, government officials broke into Entick's home with "force and arms,"

(...continued)

United States v. Jones, 14 N.C. J.L. & TECH 557, 571 (2013); David Gray & Danielle Keats Citron, *A Shattered Looking Glass: The Pitfalls and Potential of the Mosaic Theory of Fourth Amendment Privacy*, 14 N.C. J. L. & Tech. 381 (2013).

[16] ACLU v. Clapper, 959 F. Supp. 2d 724 (S.D.N.Y. 2013); Smith v. Obama, No. 2:13-CV-257 (D. Idaho June 3, 2014); *In re* Application of the Fed. Bureau of Investigation for an Order Requiring the Production of Tangible Things from [Redacted], No. BR 13-109 (FISA Ct. 2013), *available at* http://www.uscourts.gov/uscourts/courts/fisc/br13-09-primary-order.pdf.

[17] Klayman v. Obama, 957 F. Supp. 2d 1, 36 (D.D.C. 2013).

[18] Thomas K. Clancy, *What is a "Search" Within the Meaning of the Fourth Amendment*, 70 ALB. L. REV. 1, 4 (2006) ("The abhorred English and colonial search and seizure practices involved physical invasions of people's property. That was not surprising given that physical invasions were the only way authorities could intrude at the time and given the lack of technology and other sophisticated surveillance techniques."); *see generally* WILLIAM J. CUDDIHY, THE FOURTH AMENDMENT: ORIGINS AND MEANING 602-1791 (2009).

[19] *See* Thomas K. Clancy, *The Role of Individualized Suspicion in Assessing the Reasonableness of Searches and Seizures*, 25 U. MEM. L. REV. 483, 501-512 (1995) (discussing early English and American search and seizure case law).

[20] Entick v. Carrington, 95 Eng. Rep. 807, 807 (C.P. 1765).

pried open the locks on his doors, broke open his chests and drawers, and searched his private papers and books for four hours.[21] The officers conducted this search under the guise of a general warrant, a legal order which states with a high level of generality the places and things to be searched and seized. In outlawing these practices, Lord Camden of the English bench observed:

> [O]ur law holds the property of every man so sacred, that no man can set his foot upon his neighbour's close without his leave; if he does he is a trespasser, though he does no damage at all; if he will tread upon his neighbour's ground, he must justify it by law.[22]

These same intrusive practices also faced disfavor in the American colonies. British officials often resorted to writs of assistance, a form of general warrant, which permitted house-to-house searches.[23] These legal orders generally failed to allege any illegal activity and were not signed off on by a judge.[24] In the famous *Paxton's Case*, leading Boston attorney James Otis attacked these writs as "the worst instrument of arbitrary power, the most destructive of English liberty, and the fundamental principles of the constitution, that was ever found in an English law book."[25] John Adams later commented that these indiscriminate intrusions were "the spark in which originated the American Revolution."[26]

To prevent the newly established federal government from committing these incursions into their lives, the American people ratified the Fourth Amendment as part of the Bill of Rights in 1791. It reads:

> The right of the people to be secure in their persons, houses, papers, and effects, against unreasonable searches and seizures, shall not be violated, and no Warrants shall issue, but upon probable cause, supported by Oath of affirmation, and particularly describing the place to be searched, and the person or things to be seized.[27]

Over the years, the federal courts have struggled to reconcile the first clause of the Amendment, which requires that all searches and seizures be reasonable, with the second clause, which requires that all warrants meet certain minimum requirements such as particularly describing the place to be searched and the things to be seized.[28] In any event, the Court must first determine whether the Fourth Amendment's restrictions apply at all. This is done by asking whether the government has conducted a "search," a legal term of art that cannot be resolved by mere dictionary definition, but instead requires application of the Supreme Court's intricate, and at times contradictory, Fourth Amendment case law.

---

[21] *Id.*

[22] *Id.* at 817.

[23] Cuddihy, *supra* note 18, at 380.

[24] *Id.*

[25] Brief of James Otis, MASSACHUSETTS SPY, Apr. 29, 1773, at 3.

[26] 1 JOHN ADAMS & CHARLES FRANCIS ADAMS, THE WORKS OF JOHN ADAMS: SECOND PRESIDENT OF THE UNITED STATES 57 (1856).

[27] U.S. CONST. amend. IV.

[28] *See* Scott E. Sundby, *A Return to Fourth Amendment Basics: Undoing the Mischief of* Camara *and* Terry, 72 MINN. L. REV. 383, 383-84 (1988).

Early Definitions of a Fourth Amendment "Search"

Although the Fourth Amendment was ratified in 1791, the Supreme Court's first in-depth interpretation of what constitutes a Fourth Amendment search did not arise until the 1886 case *United States v. Boyd.*[29] In *Boyd*, the government obtained a court order for the Boyds to provide an invoice of goods they imported which the government planned to use against them in court. The Boyds produced the invoice, but protested that its production constituted an unreasonable search and seizure under the Fourth Amendment. Looking to *Entick* and other pre-Revolutionary cases for guidance, the Court found that the production of private papers was so similar to an actual invasion into one's home that it constituted a Fourth Amendment search.[30]

Although *Boyd* instructed that the Fourth Amendment should be "liberally construed,"[31] the Court narrowed the scope of what constitutes a search in *Olmstead v. United States.*[32] In that case, federal agents investigating the bootlegging activities of a criminal syndicate placed a wiretap on several phone lines running from the homes and office of four suspects. At no point did the officers trespass upon the defendants' property to conduct the tap. The Court held that these wiretaps should not be considered a search as the "Amendment itself shows that the search is to be of material things—the person, house, papers, and effects," and the intangible voice of the defendants was not covered by its literal terms. The Court further found that the agents did not engage in "an actual physical invasion" of Olmstead's home for purposes of conducting the wiretap.[33] Dissenting in *Olmstead*, Justice Brandeis observed that in the past, most notably in *Boyd*, the Court "refused to place an unduly literal construction" upon the Fourth Amendment.[34] Instead, he continued:

> The protection guaranteed by the amendment[] is much broader in scope. The makers of our Constitution ... sought to protect Americans in their beliefs, their thoughts, their emotions and their sensations. They conferred, as against the government, the right to be let alone-the most comprehensive of rights and the right most valued by civilized men. To protect, that right, every unjustifiable intrusion by the government upon the privacy of the individual, whatever the means employed, must be deemed a violation of the Fourth Amendment.[35]

Nonetheless, in the ensuing years, the Court assessed whether there was a search based on whether a physical trespass occurred. For instance, it was not considered a search when police engaged in eavesdropping absent a trespass.[36] However, where the police trespassed upon the suspect's property—even by an inch—the Court held that the Fourth Amendment applied.[37] Forty years later the Court would expressly overrule *Olmstead*'s literal, trespass-based interpretation of the Fourth Amendment for a privacy-based test.

---

[29] United States v. Boyd, 116 U.S. 616 (1886).

[30] *Id.*

[31] *Id.*

[32] Olmstead v. United States, 277 U.S. 438 (1928).

[33] *Id.* at 466.

[34] *Id.* at 476 (Brandeis, J, dissenting).

[35] *Id.* at 478 (Brandeis, J, dissenting).

[36] Goldman v. United States, 316 U.S. 129, 135 (1942).

[37] Silverman v. United States, 365 U.S. 505, 511-12 (1961).

Reasonable Expectation of Privacy and the Secrecy Model of Privacy

In 1967, the Court decided *Katz v. United States*, which abandoned the literal interpretation of the Fourth Amendment—one that protected only persons, houses, papers, and effects—to one that also protected intangible interests such as privacy.[38] However, while the Court sought to expand what the Fourth Amendment protects, certain passages in *Katz* simultaneously foreclosed protection for anything a person exposes to the public or another person. This would have significant consequences for government access to records and other information held by third parties.

In *Katz*, the FBI was investigating the illegal gambling activities of Mr. Katz. The FBI had attached an electronic eavesdropping device to the outside of the telephone booth in which Katz made calls and offered evidence of these calls against Katz at his prosecution. Quite sensibly, the parties framed the question presented in light of *Olmstead*'s physical trespass theory, the controlling Fourth Amendment theory of the day. They debated whether a telephone booth was a "constitutionally protected area" such that attaching the listening device to its outside would constitute a Fourth Amendment search.[39] The Court, speaking through Justice Stewart, looked beyond this traditional inquiry into protected areas, and instead declared that the "Fourth Amendment protects people, not places."[40] He observed that the "Amendment protects individual privacy against certain kinds of governmental intrusion," but also instructed that it "cannot be translated into a general constitutional 'right to privacy[.]'" Such a "right to be let alone by other people" is left largely to protection under state law.[41] In bypassing *Olmstead* and formulating the scope of the Fourth Amendment in light of privacy principles, it became necessary for the Court to lay down a rule to determine which privacy interests would be protected and which would not. Unfortunately, the majority provided little by way of guidance on the scope of this rule, beyond to say that what a person "seeks to preserve as private, even in an area accessible to the public, may be constitutionally protected" and that the use of the electronic eavesdropping device violated Katz's privacy, upon which he "justifiably relied."[42] Concurring, Justice Harlan developed a two-part framework for answering this question, which would become *Katz*'s controlling test.[43] Under Justice Harlan's formulation, a court first asks whether the person exhibited an actual or subjective expectation of privacy and second whether society is likely to deem that expectation reasonable.[44]

Beyond its general assertion that the Fourth Amendment protects people, not places, the majority made an equally far-reaching observation that "[w]hat a person knowingly exposes to the public, even in his own home or office, is not a subject of Fourth Amendment protection."[45] This rule

---

[38] Katz v. United States, 389 U.S. 347 (1967).

[39] *Id.* at 349.

[40] *Id.* at 351.

[41] *Id.* at 350.

[42] *Id.* at 351, 353.

[43] *Id.* at 360 (Harlan, J., concurring); *see* Kyllo v. United States, 533 U.S. 27, 32-33 (2001) ("In assessing when a search is not a search, we have applied somewhat in reverse the principle first enunciated in *Katz v. United States.* ... As Justice Harlan's oft-quoted concurrence described it, a Fourth Amendment search occurs when the government violates a subjective expectation of privacy that society recognizes as reasonable.").

[44] *Id.* at 361 (Harlan, J. concurring).

[45] *Katz*, 389 U.S. at 351-52.

adopts what can be called the secrecy model of privacy. Under the secrecy model, once a fact is disclosed to the public in any way, the information is no longer entitled to privacy protection.[46] This secrecy model, along with the assumption of the risk theory discussed below, would form the underpinnings of the modern third-party doctrine.

Third-Party Doctrine Jurisprudence

The idea that what a person knowingly exposes to the public is not entitled to constitutional protection was not an invention of the *Katz* court, but was embedded in Fourth Amendment jurisprudence for quite some time. In one of the first Fourth Amendment cases, *Ex parte Jackson*, the Court held that anything "exposed" on the outside of a parcel of mail is not entitled to Fourth Amendment protection.[47] Similarly, under what has come to be known as the "plain view" doctrine, Justice Brandeis noted in the 1927 case *United States v. Lee* that the use of a searchlight to view cases of liquor on the deck of a ship was not a Fourth Amendment search.[48] More prominently, the Court decided a series of cases throughout the 20th century holding that people do not have a reasonable expectation that a person with whom they are conversing will not later reveal that conversation to the police. The third-party doctrine would later be extended to documents and transactional data shared with third parties.

Undercover Informant Cases

In a series of five cases throughout the 20th century, the Supreme Court assessed the constitutionality of the use of undercover agents or informants under the Fourth Amendment. In *On Lee v. United States*, the government wired an "undercover agent" with a microphone and sent him into On Lee's laundromat to engage him in incriminating conversation.[49] An agent of the Bureau of Narcotics sat outside with a receiving set to hear the conversation. In the course of these conversations, On Lee made incriminating statements, which the agent later testified to at On Lee's trial. On Lee argued that this evidence was obtained in violation of the Fourth Amendment. In an opinion authored by Justice Jackson, the Court disagreed, noting that On Lee was "talking confidentially and indiscreetly with one he trusted" and that the agent was let into his shop "with the consent, if not implied invitation" of On Lee.[50]

In a similar case, *Lopez v. United States*, the defendant attempted to bribe an internal revenue agent, who during some of these conversations was wearing a recording device.[51] At trial, Lopez moved to suppress evidence of the wire recordings as fruits of an unlawful search. Relying on the *On Lee* decision, the Court rejected this argument on the grounds that the defendant consented to the agent being in his office and "knew full well" that the statements he made to the agent could

---

[46] Solove, *supra* note 11, at 8.

[47] *Ex parte* Jackson, 96 U.S. 727, 736 (1877).

[48] *See* United States v. Lee, 274 U.S. 559 (1927); *see also* United States v. Martin, 806 F.2d 204, 207 (8th Cir. 1986) ("[I]t was inappropriate to subject the agent's conduct of looking through the window of the truck to Fourth Amendment scrutiny in the first place. The agent's mere observation of gun parts left in plain view on the front seat of the truck did not implicate any Fourth Amendment rights.").

[49] On Lee v. United States, 343 U.S. 747, 748 (1952).

[50] *Id.* at 751-52.

[51] Lopez v. United States, 373 U.S. 427, 430 (1963).

be used against him.[52] Further, the Court noted that the listening device was not used to intercept conversations the agent could not have otherwise heard, but "instead, the device was used only to obtain the most reliable evidence possible of a conversation in which the Government's own agent was a participant and which that agent was fully entitled to disclose."[53]

In *Lewis v. United States*, the government sent an undercover federal narcotics agent to the defendant's home several times to purchase marijuana.[54] Over the defendant's objections, the agent was permitted to recount the conversations at trial. Upon review, the Supreme Court held that the conversations were not protected under the Fourth Amendment as the defendant had invited the federal agent into his home and that the statements were "willingly" made to the agent.[55]

Finally, in *Hoffa v. United States*, a government informant relayed to federal law enforcement agents the many conversations he had with Jimmy Hoffa about Hoffa's attempt to tamper with a jury.[56] Because the informant did not enter Hoffa's hotel room by force, was invited to participate in the conversations by Hoffa, and was not a "surreptitious eavesdropper," the Court concluded that the Fourth Amendment had not been violated.[57]

There appear to be two motivating principles underlying these undercover informant cases. In one sense, the Court was applying *Olmstead*'s physical invasion test: because the informants had not trespassed into the defendants' homes or offices—in the words of pre-*Katz* case law, their "constitutionally protected areas"—there could be no constitutional invasion.[58] Rather, in each instance, the informant was invited onto the premises. For example, in *On Lee*, the Court observed that On Lee could not raise the issue of trespass as he had consented, if not invited, the agent to enter his business. A claim of trespass could only be made if the agent had entered by force or by show of authority.[59] In another sense, the Court found that voluntarily telling another person something gave him consent to share that information with another person including the government.[60] For instance, *Hoffa* instructed that the Fourth Amendment does not protect "a wrongdoer's misplaced belief that a person to whom he voluntarily confides his wrongdoing will not reveal it."[61]

Note that these cases came before *Katz* shifted the Fourth Amendment focus from property to privacy. Whether *Katz* would disturb this line of cases was a matter of "considerable

---

[52] *Id.* at 437.

[53] *Id.* at 439.

[54] Lewis v. United States, 385 U.S. 206 (1966).

[55] *Id* at 210, 212.

[56] Hoffa v. United States, 385 U.S. 293, 296 (1966).

[57] *Id.* at 302.

[58] *See Lopez*, 373 U.S. at 439 ("And the device was not planted by means of an unlawful physical invasion of petitioner's premises under circumstances that would violate the Fourth Amendment.").

[59] *See* On Lee, 343 U.S. at 751-52.

[60] *Hoffa*, 385 U.S. at 302 ("[The government agent] was in the suite by invitation, and every conversation which he heard was either directed to him or knowingly carried on in his presence."); *Lopez*, 373 U.S. at 438 ("The only evidence obtained consisted of statements made by the [defendant] to the [government agent], statements which [the defendant] knew full well could be used against him by [the government agent] if he wished.").

[61] *Hoffa*, 385 U.S. at 302.

speculation"[62] until the Court decided *United States v. White* four years later. In *White*, an undercover informant wearing a radio transmitter engaged the defendant in several incriminating conversations, four of which took place at the informant's house, and several other conversations took place in the defendant's home, a restaurant, and in the informant's car.[63] The court of appeals in *White* interpreted *Katz* as implicitly overruling this line of cases as it was based on a trespass doctrine that was "squarely discarded" in *Katz*.[64] The Supreme Court disagreed, however, and upheld the surreptitious surveillance. The opinion accepted that the trespass rationale could not survive after *Katz*, but that the undercover informant cases were also supported by a "second and independent ground"—that the informant was not an uninvited eavesdropper, but a party to the conversation who was free to report what he heard to the authorities.[65] For the Court, White had assumed the risk that information he shared with the informant could be shared with the police.[66]

With *White*, the Court combined several ideas in its Fourth Amendment jurisprudence: first, that it is unreasonable for people to expect privacy in information they share with another, and second, that they assume the risk that that information can be handed over to the government.[67] With these two theories in mind, the Court resolved two major third-party doctrine cases in the 1970s, *United States v. Miller* and *Smith v. Maryland*.[68] These cases would become the cornerstone of the modern third-party doctrine, and have been heavily relied upon by government officials to access various types of transactional data without a search warrant.

Miller v. United States—Subpoena for Bank Records

In 1976, the Court took up its first major third-party doctrine case to deal with transactional documents in *Miller v. United States*. In that case, agents of the Treasury Department's Alcohol, Tobacco, and Firearms Bureau were investigating Mitch Miller for his participation in an illegal whiskey distillery.[69] The agents subpoenaed the presidents of several banks in which Miller had an account to produce all records of accounts including savings, checking accounts, and any loans he may have had. The banks never informed Miller that the subpoenas had been served, but ordered their employees to comply with the subpoenas. At one bank, an agent was shown

---

[62] *See* 1 WAYNE R. LAFAVE, SEARCH AND SEIZURE § 2.2(f) (2004).

[63] United States v. White, 401 U.S. 745, 746-47 (1971).

[64] United States v. White, 405 F.2d 838 (7th Cir. 1969).

[65] *White*, 401 U.S. at 750 (quoting *On Lee*, 343 U.S. at 753-54) ("It would be a dubious service to the genuine liberties protected by the Fourth Amendment to make them bedfellows with spurious liberties improvised by farfetched analogies which would liken eavesdropping on a conversation, with the connivance of one of the parties, to an unreasonable search or seizure.")).

[66] *Id.* at 752 ("Inescapably, one contemplating illegal activities must realize that his companions may be reporting to the police."). Assumption of the risk is more commonly found in the context of tort law, where a person assumes certain risks that accompany the activities he is engaged in. *See* Murphy v. Steeplechase Amusements Co., 250 N.Y. 479 (1929) (Cardozo, J.) ("Volenti non fit injuria. One who takes part in such a sport accepts the dangers that inhere in it so far as they are obvious and necessary, just as a fencer accepts the risk of a thrust by his antagonist or a spectator at a ball game the chance of contact with the ball.").

[67] While primarily concerned with the Fifth Amendment right to self-incrimination, *Couch v. United States*, 409 U.S. 322, 335(1973), observed that "there can be little expectation of privacy where [tax] records are handed to an accountant, knowing that mandatory disclosure of much of the information therein is required in an income tax return.").

[68] United States v. Miller, 425 U.S. 435 (1976); Smith v. Maryland, 442 U.S. 735 (1979).

[69] *Miller*, 425 U.S. at 437.

microfilm of Miller's account and provided copies of "one deposit slip and one or two checks."[70] At the other bank, the agent was shown similar records and was given copies of "all checks, deposit slips, two financial statements, and three monthly statements."[71] Copies of the checks were later introduced into evidence at Miller's trial.

The lower court held that the government had unlawfully circumvented the Fourth Amendment by first requiring the banks to maintain the customer's records for a certain period of time and second by using insufficient legal process to obtain those records from the bank. In a 7-2 ruling, the Supreme Court reversed and held that subpoenaing the bank records without a warrant did not violate the Fourth Amendment. The opinion by Justice Powell discarded the first argument by noting that previous case law held that merely requiring the bank to retain its customers' records did not constitute a Fourth Amendment search.[72] That previous case, however, did not resolve whether a subpoena was sufficient to access those documents.[73] Miller argued that the bank kept copies of personal records that he gave to the bank for a limited purpose and in which he retained a reasonable expectation of privacy under *Katz*. The Court, applying language from *Katz*, noted that "[w]hat a person knowingly exposes to the public ... is not a subject of Fourth Amendment protection."[74] The Court concluded that banking documents were not "confidential communications," but rather negotiable instruments that were required to transact business between the customer and the bank. All of the documents contained information "voluntarily conveyed to the banks and exposed to their employees in the ordinary course of business."[75] As with the undercover agent cases, once documents were shared with the bank, they could then be given to the government without requiring a search warrant. Citing to *White*, Justice Powell instructed that a bank customer "takes the risk, in revealing his affairs to another, that the information will be conveyed by that person to the government."[76] Looking to both this assumption of the risk theory and the secrecy model, the Court then included the following sentence which would come to encapsulate the third-party doctrine:

> This Court has held repeatedly that the Fourth Amendment does not prohibit the obtaining of information revealed to a third party and conveyed by him to Government authorities, even if the information is revealed on the assumption that it will be used only for a limited purpose and the confidence placed in the third party will not be betrayed.[77]

Based on this assertion, Miller could have no reasonable expectation of privacy in the bank records and thus the introduction of them at his prosecution did not contravene the Fourth Amendment.

---

[70] *Id.* at 438.

[71] *Id.*

[72] *Miller*, 425 U.S. at 441 (quoting California Bankers Assn. v. Shultz, 416 U.S. 21, 54 (1974)).

[73] *See California Bankers Ass'n*, 416 U.S. at 54 n.24.

[74] *Miller*, 425 U.S. at 442 (quoting Katz v. United States, 389 U.S. 347, 351 (1967)).

[75] *Id.*

[76] *Id.* at 443.

[77] *Id.* at 443.

Smith v. Maryland—Subpoena for Telephone Call Records

Several years later, the Court took up the second major third-party doctrine case, *Smith v. Maryland*,[78] which would have major implications for government collection of transactional records, especially those held by third-party companies.

In *Smith*, the police were investigating the robbery of a young woman, who gave the police a description of her assailant and the vehicle seen near the scene of the crime.[79] The police later spotted a man matching the victim's description driving an identical vehicle in her neighborhood, which they traced back to Michael Smith. Upon police request, the telephone company installed a pen register at its central office to record the telephone numbers dialed from Smith's home. The device was installed without a warrant or court order. Through the pen register, the police learned that a call was placed from Smith's home to the victim's phone, which would eventually connect Smith to the robbery. At trial, Smith claimed that any evidence obtained from the pen register violated his Fourth Amendment rights as the police failed to obtain a warrant before installing it. This motion was denied, Smith was later convicted of robbery, and the appeals court affirmed his conviction, holding that the installation of the pen register was not a Fourth Amendment search.[80]

In line with Justice Harlan's formulation of the *Katz* privacy test, the Supreme Court asked the following questions: first, whether Smith had a subjective expectation of privacy in the numbers he dialed, and second, whether that expectation was reasonable.[81] As to the former, the Court "doubt[ed] that people in general entertain any actual expectation of privacy in the numbers they dial."[82] The Court assumed that people, in the main, know and understand that they must convey the dialed numbers to the company to complete the call; that the company has a process of recording those numbers; and that the company actually does record those numbers for various business reasons. It deduced this partially from the fact that phone books inform consumers that the telephone companies "can frequently help in identifying to authorities the origin of unwelcome and untroublesome calls" and that customers see a list of their calls recorded on their monthly phone bills.[83]

Even if *Smith* did harbor a subjective expectation of privacy, the Court found that "this expectation is not 'one society is prepared to recognize as 'reasonable.'"[84] Justice Blackmun cited to *Miller*, *White*, *Hoffa*, and *Lopez* for the proposition that "a person has no legitimate expectation of privacy in information that he voluntarily turns over to third parties."[85] Because Smith "voluntarily conveyed" the telephone numbers to the company in the process of making the call, he had "exposed" that information to the company's equipment in the "ordinary course of business" and thus could not reasonably expect privacy in that information.[86] Moreover, the Court

---

[78] Smith v. Maryland, 442 U.S. 735 (1979).

[79] *Id.* at 737.

[80] Smith v. Maryland, 283 Md. 156, 173 (1978).

[81] *Smith*, 442 U.S. at 740.

[82] *Id.* at 742.

[83] *Id.* at 742-43

[84] *Id.* at 743 (quoting *Katz*, 389 U.S. at 361).

[85] *Id.* at 743-44.

[86] *Id.* at 744.

found that Smith "assumed the risk" that the telephone company would reveal to the police the numbers he dialed.[87]

Although *Smith* was the Court's last significant pronouncement on the parameters of the third-party doctrine, the lower federal courts have applied it in various contexts, with a significant number of these cases dealing with the transfer of electronic information.

Other Applications of the Third-Party Doctrine

After *Miller* and *Smith*, the courts have applied the third-party doctrine to a host of various scenarios including metadata connected to Internet communications, cell phone location information, and utility billing records, among others. These cases generally divide along a content/non-content distinction: the content of a communication, such as the body of an email, does not fall within third-party doctrine, and other Fourth Amendment rules apply. Addressing information, such as the to/from line in an email, the outside of a letter, or the telephone numbers dialed, however, are covered by the doctrine. There have been various rationales for this divide, the most compelling being the difference between the recipient of the information and companies that act merely as a conduit or intermediary between two people communicating with each other.

The difference in constitutional treatment between the content of a communication and its non-content addressing information dates at least as far back as the 19th century. In the 1877 case *Ex parte Jackson*, the Supreme Court held that the content of a mailed letter was protected under the Fourth Amendment, while the information exposed to the public, such as the address written on the outside, was not.[88] This dichotomy was further developed in *Katz* and *Smith*. In *Katz*, the Court protected the content of Mr. Katz's communication (his voice), noting that a caller is "surely entitled to assume that the words he utters into the mouthpiece will not be broadcast to the world."[89] *Non*-content information was not before the Court in *Katz*. On the other hand, *Smith* left non-content information, the numbers he dialed, unprotected, as pen registers do not allow law enforcement to "hear sound" and "[n]either the purport of any communication between the caller and the recipient of the call, their identities, nor whether the call was even completed is disclosed[.]"[90]

This distinction between content and non-content has also been applied in the lower courts. In *United States v. Warshak*, the Sixth Circuit Court of Appeals held that individuals enjoy a reasonable expectation of privacy in the *content* of their emails.[91] The panel noted that "email requires strong protection under the Fourth Amendment; otherwise, the Fourth Amendment would prove an ineffective guardian of private communication, an essential purpose it has long been recognized to serve."[92] Following *Smith*'s lead, the courts have taken the opposite approach to non-content or addressing information that accompanies an email or other electronic

---

[87] *Id.*

[88] *Ex parte* Jackson, 96 U.S. 727, 733 (1877); *see also* United States v. Jacobsen, 466 U.S. 109, 114 (1984) ("Letters and other sealed packages are in the general class of effects in which the public at large has a legitimate expectation of privacy; warrantless searches of such effects are presumptively unreasonable").

[89] Katz v. United States, 389 U.S. 347, 352 (1967).

[90] *Smith*, 442 U.S. at 741 (quoting United States v. New York Tel. Co. 434 U.S. 159, 167 (1977)).

[91] United States v. Warshak, 631 F.3d 266, 288 (6th Cir. 2010); *see also* City of Ontario v. Quon, 560 U.S. 746, 757 (2010) (assuming that petitioner had reasonable expectation of privacy in content of emails).

[92] *Id.* at 286.

communications. In *United States v. Forrester*, for example, the Ninth Circuit Court of Appeals held that the to/from addresses of emails, the IP addresses of websites a person visits, and the total volume of data transmitted to or from a certain account were not subject to Fourth Amendment protection.[93] The Ninth Circuit found that like the telephone numbers in *Smith*, email and Internet users should know that addressing information "is provided to and used by Internet Service Providers (ISP) for the specific purpose of directing the routing of information."[94] Moreover, the court noted that although the government can make an "educated guess" about what was said in a message or viewed on a particular website, this information does not "necessarily reveal any more about the underlying contents of the communication than do phone numbers."[95] Further emphasizing this distinction, while *Smith* covered the telephone numbers a person dials to make a call, government access to the numbers dialed after a call has been placed, known as "post-cut through dialed digits," is considered a Fourth Amendment search.[96] These numbers, which might include "bank account numbers, Social Security numbers, prescription numbers, and the like," constitute the "contents of communications" and are "the kind of information that an individual wants and reasonably expects to be kept private."[97]

Another dividing line between protected and unprotected information pertains to the identity of the service provider in the chain of communication. If the provider is seen as a party to the transaction and is a *recipient* of the information, the records are generally considered "business records" of that company and subject to the third-party doctrine. This rationale is similar to that applied in the undercover informant cases. Although the information provided to an informant constitutes the content of the communication, it is not protected because it was spoken directly to the agent—in other words, the agent was the *recipient* of that information. Alternatively, where the company merely acts as a *conduit* or *intermediary* and "passively convey[s]" that information to an end-user, the material is generally not subject to the third-party doctrine.[98]

In *Warshak*, the Sixth Circuit noted that the ISP was acting as an "intermediary that makes email communication possible."[99] Just like the post office which acts as an intermediary of a letter, and the telephone company which acts as an intermediary to the voice content of phone calls, "emails must pass through an ISP's server to reach their intended recipient."[100] And just as the police are prohibited from accessing communications from the post office or a telephone company without first obtaining a warrant, the Sixth Circuit held that a warrant should equally be required to access more modern forms of communications.[101] Distinguishing the bank records case *Miller*, the court found that whereas the bank records, checks, and deposit slips in *Miller* were given directly to the

---

[93] United States v. Forrester, 512 F.3d 500, 510 (9th Cir. 2007).

[94] *Id.* at 510.

[95] *Id.*

[96] See *In Re* of Applications of the United States of America for Orders (1) Authorizing the Use of Pen Registers and Trap and Trace Devices and (2) Authorizing Release of Subscriber Information, 515 F. Supp. 2d 325, 339 (E.D.N.Y. 2007); *see also In re* Application of the United States of America for an Order Authorizing (1) Installation and Use of a Pen Register and Trap and Trace Device or Process, (2) Access to Customer Records, and (3) Cell Phone Tracking, 441 F. Supp. 2d 816, (S.D. Tex. 2006) (deciding case on statutory grounds but noting constitutional concern with access to post-cut-through dialed digits without a warrant based upon probable cause).

[97] *In re Application for Subscriber Information*, 515 F. Supp. 2d at 336.

[98] *Forrester*, 512 F.3d at 510.

[99] *Warshak*, 631 F.3d at 286.

[100] *Id.*

[101] *Id.*

banks to be used in the "ordinary course of business," the ISP was the "intermediary, not the intended recipient of the emails."[102] The court rejected the government's arguments that the "ability" and "right" of the ISP to access emails stored on its servers should eliminate any Fourth Amendment privacy interests, as a similar ability of the telephone operators in *Katz* to listen in on conversations carried over their system did not eliminate a user's reasonable expectation of privacy.[103]

Another prominent example of this conduit versus recipient dichotomy can be found in lower federal court cases treating cell location data as a business record not subject to Fourth Amendment protection. In a 2013 Fifth Circuit Court of Appeals case, the government sought access to two months of historical cell site location data, which provides the location of a cell phone based on its proximity to the nearest cell tower.[104] Noting this distinction between intermediary and recipient, the court found that cell site records are "clearly business records" for which the third-party doctrine should apply, as the cell provider is a party to the transaction; the location information is not transferred to anyone but the provider; and the location information is needed to route the call.[105] Like the Fifth Circuit, several lower courts have applied the third-party doctrine to hold that access to cell site location information is not a Fourth Amendment search.[106]

However, over the past several years, a growing number of judges have pushed back against government attempts to circumvent the Fourth Amendment warrant requirement when seeking information about an individual's cell phone location data. The District Court for the Eastern District of New York, for instance, found that while the third-party doctrine generally covers the type of location information produced by a cell phone call, the "cumulative" collection of 113 days of constant surveillance implicated sufficiently heightened privacy interests to warrant an exception to the third-party doctrine.[107] This argument is based on the "mosaic theory" of the Fourth Amendment, which holds that while short-term monitoring may not reveal anything overly private about an individual, the aggregation of this information can be much more revealing.[108] In an alternative approach, the Third Circuit Court of Appeals reasoned that a cell phone user does not "voluntarily" share his location with a cell phone provider "in any meaningful way," prohibiting application of the third-party doctrine, but held that it was left to the discretion of the magistrate judge whether a warrant would be required.[109]

A more recent legal problem facing the lower courts is determining whether the third-party doctrine should apply to "cell tower dumps." These are instances in which the government is looking for the cell phone records of *unknown* persons who may have made a cell phone call after

---

[102] *Id.* at 288.

[103] *Id.* (emphasis in original).

[104] *In re* Application of the United States of America for Historical Cell Site Data, 724 F.3d 600, 602 (5th Cir. 2013).

[105] *Id.* at 612.

[106] *See, e.g., In re* Application of the United States of America for an Order for Disclosure of Telecommunications Records and Authorizing the Use of a Pen Register and Trap and Trace, 405 F. Supp. 2d 435, 449-50 (S.D.N.Y. 2005); United States v. Graham, 846 F. Supp. 2d 384, 403 (D. Mar. 2012); United States v. Benford, No. 2:09-CR-86, 2010 WL 1266507 (N.D. Ind. 2010).

[107] *In re* Application of the United States of America for an Order Authorizing the Release of Historical Cell-Site Information, 809 F. Supp. 2d 113, 126 (E.D.N.Y. 2011).

[108] See *infra* "Implications of *United States v. Jones* on the Third-Party Doctrine," pp. 21-23.

[109] *See In re* Application of the United States of America for an Order Directing a Provider of Electronic Communication Service to Disclose Records to the Government, 620 F.3d 304, 317-18 (3d 2010).

a reported crime, say, a bank robbery. The government requests all the calls made from the nearest cell tower within a certain period of time.[110] The few courts that have addressed the issue have split on whether a warrant is required.[111] Thus far, the reasoning in these cases has not been fully developed.

Beyond the specific factors the courts have used to determine whether the third-party doctrine should apply (e.g., content versus non-content, intermediary versus recipient), there have been both doctrinal and practical arguments made for and against its very existence.

Support for the Third-Party Doctrine

Perhaps the strongest argument in support of the third-party doctrine is its ability to be harmonized with the rest of Fourth Amendment case law. One only has to quickly scan the Supreme Court Reporter to realize that the third-party doctrine is consistent with numerous other cases which hold that acts or things revealed to the public are not entitled to Fourth Amendment protection.

Take, for instance, the garbage collection case, *California v. Greenwood*.[112] There, the police requested that a trash collector pick up a suspect's plastic trash bags left in front of his house so the officer could search it for contraband or other evidence of criminal activity. The Court concluded that the defendant was not entitled to a reasonable expectation of privacy in his trash as he discarded it where it could be accessed by the public.[113] Similarly, in *United States v. Knotts*, the Court held that a person does not have a legitimate privacy expectation in his public movements as he voluntarily conveys this information to anyone who wants to look.[114] This theory has also been applied to cases where police flew an airplane 1,000 feet and a helicopter 400 feet over private property in search of illegal activity.[115] The rationale in those cases was that any member of the public flying in federally regulated airspace could have looked down and seen what the officers saw, vitiating any privacy expectation in that space.[116] In *United States v. Jacobsen*, the Court held that it was not a search when police opened a mailed package after its contents had already been viewed by an employee of a private freight carrier.[117] There, the Court observed that once the defendant's privacy expectation had been frustrated by one person, it became public information subject to government investigation.[118]

---

[110] *See* Brian L. Owsley, *The Fourth Amendment Implications of the Government's Use of Cell Tower Dumps in Its Electronic Surveillance*, 16 U. PA. J. CONST. L. 1, 1-2 (2013).

[111] *Compare In re* Application of the United States of America for an Order Pursuant to 18 U.S.C. § 2703(d), 964 F. Supp. 2d 674, 678 (denying access to cell tower dump records) *with* United States v. Capito, No. 3:10-CR-8050 (D. Ariz Sept 14, 2011) (upholding access to cell tower dump records).

[112] California v. Greenwood, 486 U.S. 35, 37 (1988).

[113] *Id.* at 42.

[114] United States v. Knotts, 460 U.S. 276, 281-82 (1983).

[115] California v. Ciraolo, 476 U.S. 207, 213-14 (1986) (airplane); Florida v. Riley, 488 U.S. 445, 455 (1989) (helicopter).

[116] *Ciraolo*, 476 U.S. at 213-214; *Riley*, 488 U.S. at 451.

[117] United States v. Jacobsen, 466 U.S. 109, 117-18 (1984).

[118] *Id.* at 117. Like the Fourth Amendment, under the privacy tort of intrusion upon seclusion, which subjects one to liability for intruding upon the solitude or seclusion of another, there is no liability for observing or taking a person's photograph in public for his appearance is "open to the public eye." RESTATEMENT (SECOND) OF TORTS § 652B cmt. b (continued...)

As a more practical matter, assistance from third parties is utilized by law enforcement in almost every investigation. When investigating a murder, robbery, or any other crime committed in the real world, police officers will usually interview witnesses to obtain facts about the crime. To conduct these interviews, the officers generally need not obtain a warrant, and witnesses who refuse to cooperate can be compelled to testify with a grand jury subpoena.[119] It could be argued that this process of fact finding is very similar to requesting documentary evidence held by third parties and the same standard should be applied to each.

In this same vein, Professor Orin Kerr has defended the third-party doctrine on the ground that it maintains the appropriate balance of privacy and security in the face of technological change.[120] Without the ability to use third parties such as telephone or Internet companies, Kerr posits, the criminal would traditionally have to go out into the public to commit his crime where the Fourth Amendment offers more limited protection. He argues that a criminal can use the services of these third parties to commit crimes without having to expose these activities to areas open to public surveillance.[121] This, he posits, upsets the privacy-security balance that undergirds the Fourth Amendment because it would require police to have probable cause to obtain any evidence of the crime: "The effect would be a Catch-22: The police would need probable cause to observe evidence of the crime, but they would need to observe evidence of the crime first to get probable cause."[122] Kerr contends that the third-party doctrine responds to this imbalance by providing the same amount of protection regardless of whether the defendant commits the crime on his own or through the use of a third-party service.

From an institutional perspective, one might argue that the courts are not the proper branch of the federal government to resolve privacy disputes related to information handed over to third-parties. Once the Supreme Court outlaws, or significantly limits, a certain police practice, it "constitutionalizes" it, and only the Court or a constitutional amendment could overturn this decision. Instead, some argue that when creating rules that pertain to new technologies, Congress, and legislatures generally, might be best fitted to find the appropriate balance between privacy and security, while providing the necessary flexibility to change this rule as technology changes.[123]

Another argument in support of the third-party doctrine is that the companies which hold a person's records "own" them, as they are in possession of them and are generally the ones that create them.[124] Once possessed by the company, the argument runs, it can transfer these documents to others free from the permission of the subject of the documents. The Court relied on this theory in *Miller*, where it noted that the bank records were not the defendant's "private

---

(...continued)

(2013).

[119] United States v. Dionisio, 410 U.S. 1, 9-10 (1973) (observing the "historically grounded obligation of every person to appear and give his evidence before the grand jury. 'The personal sacrifice involved is a part of the necessary contribution of the individual to the welfare of the public.' And while the duty may be 'onerous' at times, it is 'necessary to the administration of justice.'").

[120] *See* Orin Kerr, *The Case for the Third Party Doctrine*, 107 MICH. L. REV. 561, 575 (2009).

[121] *Id.*

[122] *Id.* at 576.

[123] *See* Orin Kerr, *The Fourth Amendment and New Technologies: Constitutional Myths and the Case for Caution*, 102 MICH. L. REV. 801, 859 (2004).

[124] Slobogin, *supra* note 7, at 157 (describing arguments for and against the possessory interest argument).

---

papers," and as such he could "assert neither ownership nor possession."[125] Instead, they were deemed "the business records of the banks."[126] This argument is buttressed by the theory that the First Amendment protects a person's right to communicate facts to others.[127]

Criticism of the Third-Party Doctrine

While the third-party doctrine appears to fit reasonably well with the rest of Fourth Amendment case law, and has other weighty arguments in its favor, it has also had its share of vocal critics both on and off the Court. There have been four major arguments against its application: (1) privacy is not an all-or-nothing proposition that is lost once information is disclosed to another person or company; (2) information sent to third-party companies is not actually "voluntary," as people need these services to participate in modern society; (3) the judiciary should not impose privacy regimes on the citizenry without engaging in a more comprehensive privacy analysis; and (4) failing to protect information shared with others has the potential to breed distrust among people or businesses communicating with each other.

The first major argument against the third-party doctrine challenges the notion that once privacy is lost to one person, it is lost to the world. At bottom, this is a challenge to the secrecy model of the Fourth Amendment. The secrecy theory of privacy has been criticized for not taking into consideration that people may not want to engage in "total disclosure" of information they share with others, but instead seek to selectively disclose that information.[128] Justice Marshall said as much in dissent in *Smith v. Maryland,*where he argued that "privacy is not a discrete commodity, possessed absolutely or not at all."[129] He continued: "Those who disclose certain facts to a bank or phone company for a limited business purpose need not assume that this information will be released to other persons for other purposes."[130] Several commentators have similarly argued that there is an important distinction between information that is broadcast to the world and that which is disclosed in a controlled environment.[131] The first category, they argue, includes instances where the government accesses information that is readily available in the public square, such as information posted on a publicly available website or a loud conversation overheard in an airport.[132] Because the person has decided to release this information to the public, he cannot later claim to have an expectation of privacy. The latter category, on the other hand, entails a more limited sharing that is "an integral part of a legitimate transaction" between the individual and the recipient of the information, and is entitled to Fourth Amendment protection.[133]

---

[125] United States v. Miller, 425 U.S. 435, 440-41 (1976)

[126] *Id.*

[127] *See* Eugene Volokh, *Freedom of Speech and Information Privacy: The Troubling Implications of a Right to Stop People from Speaking About You*, 52 STAN. L. REV. 1049, 1053 (2000).

[128] See *Kenneth L. Karst, "The Files": Legal Controls Over the Accuracy and Accessibility of Stored Personal Data*, 31 LAW & CONTEMP. PROBS. 342, 344 (1966).

[129] *Smith*, 442 U.S. at 749 (Marshall, J., dissenting).

[130] *Id.*

[131] Susan W. Brenner & Leo L. Clarke, *Fourth Amendment for Shared Privacy Rights in Stored Transactional Data*, 14 J.L. & POL'Y 211, 258 (2006).

[132] *Id.*

[133] *Id.* This idea that a person loses all Fourth Amendment protection in information he shares with another would seem to be undermined by various cases in which shared information or spaces did not lose constitutional protection. For instance, in *Minnesota v. Olson*, the Court held that an overnight guest could have a reasonable expectation of privacy (continued...)

Along these same lines, some have pointed out the apparent inconsistency in Fourth Amendment protection accorded to various types of information people share with third parties. In *Katz v. United States* and *Berger v. New York*, the Court held that people have an expectation of privacy in the content of their conversations,[134] while similar protection was not extended to the telephone numbers dialed in *Smith*.[135] Dissenting in *Smith,* Justice Stewart, who authored the *Katz* majority opinion, pointed out this incongruity, noting that like telephone numbers, the voice of a conversation must be transmitted through the telephone company's equipment and may be overheard or recorded by that company.[136] He argued that "what the telephone company does or might do with those numbers is no more relevant to this inquiry than it would be in a case involving the conversation itself."[137] Instead, Justice Stewart would have granted both forms of information protection under *Katz*.[138] In a line that would foreshadow more recent arguments against the third-party doctrine, Justice Stewart contended that people are not concerned about revealing a list of their telephone calls because it could be incriminating, but rather because it would "reveal the most intimate details of a person's life."[139]

The second major argument against the third-party doctrine challenges the idea that people "voluntarily" convey information to others when engaging in business transactions. In *Miller*, the Court asserted that the financial statements and deposit slips were "voluntarily conveyed" to the banks in the "ordinary course of business,"[140] and in *Smith* the defendant "voluntarily conveyed numerical information to the telephone company."[141] More recently, a federal court of appeals judge made a similar argument regarding cell phone users:

> Their use of their phones, moreover, is entirely voluntary. The Government does not require a member of the public to own or carry a phone. As the days of monopoly phone companies are past, the Government does not require him to obtain his cell phone service from a particular service provider that keeps historical cell site records for its subscribers, either. And it does not require him to make a call, let alone to make a call at a specific location.[142]

There has been significant disagreement, however, about how *voluntary* these transactions really are. Justice Brennan argued in dissent that "for all practical purposes, the disclosure by individuals or business firms of their financial affairs to a bank is not entirely volitional, since it is impossible to participate in the economic life of contemporary society without maintaining a bank account."[143] Similarly, Justice Marshall argued in *Smith* that "unless a person is prepared to forgo

---

(...continued)

in the home of his host, "a place where he and his possessions will not be disturbed by anyone but his host and those his host allows inside."[133] On the other hand, these cases took place in the context of the home, an area accorded the highest Fourth Amendment protection, and their holdings might not easily extend to other contexts.

[134] Katz v. United States, 389 U.S. 347, 353 (1967); Berger v. New York, 388 U.S. 41, 51 (1967).

[135] *Smith*, 442 U.S. at 745.

[136] *Id.* at 746 (Stewart, J., dissenting).

[137] *Id.* at 747 (1979) (Stewart, J., dissenting).

[138] *Id.*

[139] *Id.* at 748 (Stewart, J., dissenting).

[140] United States v. Miller, 425 U.S. 435, 442 (1976).

[141] *Smith*, 442 U.S. 442 U.S. 744.

[142] *In re* Application of the United States of America for Historical Cell Site Data, 724 F.3d 600, 613 (5th Cir. 2013) (internal citation omitted),

[143] United States v. Miller, 425 U.S. 435, 451 (1973) (Brennan, J., dissenting) (quoting Burrows v. Superior Court, 13 Cal. 3d 238, 247 (1974)).

use" of the telephone, which for "many has become a personal or professional necessity, he cannot help but accept the risk of surveillance. It is idle to speak of 'assuming' risks in contexts where, as a practical matter, individuals have no realistic alternative."[144] One commentator has argued that unlike the undercover agent cases, where refusing to talk to a particular individual is a "realistic option," refusing to get medical treatment or an education would lead to an "unproductive" and "possibly much foreshortened existence."[145]

The third central argument against the third-party doctrine challenges the assertion that people "assume the risk" when handing information over to third parties. People do not assume legal risks as a matter of pure deduction, the argument goes, "but assume only those risks of unregulated government intrusion that the courts tell us we have to assume."[146] Dissenting in *White*, Justice Harlan expressed concern about the process by which courts determine how much privacy protection people should expect and will receive. He notes that people's expectations of privacy and the risks they assume are "reflections" of the laws handed down by courts or legislatures. Because it is the "task of the law to form and project, as well as mirror or reflect," Justice Harlan instructs, "we should not, as judges, merely recite the expectations and risks without examining the desirability of saddling them upon society."[147] Instead of allowing "the substitution of words for analysis," courts should assess "the nature of a particular practice and the likely extent of its impact on the individual's sense of security balanced against the utility of the conduct as a technique of law enforcement."[148] In other words, rather than simply applying the phrase "assumption of the risk" in each new legal context, Justice Harlan suggested that courts should look anew at each surveillance practice and determine its actual impact on the individual's privacy interests.[149] One commentator has suggested a similar approach in that the government should not have "practically unrestricted access" to people's records, or, on the flipside, that probable cause must be required for every request of documents. Instead, he argues that the level of protection should depend on the nature of the documents requested.[150] For example, certain types of records, including public records, may not be entitled to the same protection as others, such as medical or financial records.[151]

---

[144] *Smith*, 442 U.S. at 750 (Marshall, J., dissenting).

[145] Slobogin, *supra* note 7, at 156.

[146] *Id.* at 157; *see also* Stephen E. Henderson, *The Timely Demise of the Fourth Amendment Third Party Doctrine*, 96 IOWA L. REV. BULL. 39, 47 ("It is the law that defines what risks we do and do not assume.") .

[147] *White*, 401 U.S. at 786 (Harlan, J., concurring). A similar, and more general, criticism has been posed against the *Katz* 's reasonable expectation of privacy test. Some have argued that it in determining which expectations of privacy are reasonable, judges are merely imposing their own views of privacy on society. *See* United States v. Jones, 132 S. Ct. 945, 962 (2012) (Alito, J., concurring) ("The *Katz* expectation-of-privacy test ... is not without its own difficulties. It involves a degree of circularity, and judges are apt to confuse their own expectations of privacy with those of the hypothetical reasonable person to which the *Katz* test looks."); Minnesota v. Carter, 525 U.S. 83, 97 (1998) (Scalia, J., concurring) ("In my view, the only thing the past three decades have established about the *Katz* test ... is that, unsurprisingly, those 'actual (subjective) expectation[s] of privacy' 'that society is prepared to recognize as 'reasonable,'' bear an uncanny resemblance to those expectations of privacy that this Court considers reasonable.").

[148] *United States v. White*, 401 U.S. 745, 786 (1971) (Harlan, J., concurring).

[149] *See* Catherine Hancock, *Warrants for Wearing a Wire: Fourth Amendment Privacy and Justice Harlan's Dissent in United States v. White*, 79 MISS. L. J. 35 (2009). Similar to Justice Harlan's comments, the majority in *Smith v. Maryland* observed that if people's subjective expectations of privacy becomes conditioned by government practices that were "alien to well-recognized Fourth Amendment freedoms," that a "normative inquiry would be proper" in determining what constituted a "legitimate expectation of privacy." *Smith*, 442 U.S. at 740-41 n.5.

[150] Slobogin, *supra* note 7, at 157.

[151] Slobogin, *supra* note 7, at 157.

Lastly, many practical arguments have been formulated against application of third-party doctrine. Justice Harlan believed one of the main concerns with the third-party doctrine was its ability to breed distrust in people who are communicating with others. He noted that the practice of third-party bugging "undermine[s] the confidence and sense of security in dealing with one another that is characteristic of individual relationships between citizens in a free society."[152] In Justice Harlan's view, "words would be measured a good deal more carefully and communication inhibited if one suspected his conversations were being transmitted and transcribed."[153] One only has to look to the recent NSA controversy as a more modern example. Some argue that knowledge that information shared with tech companies like Google, Facebook, and Apple might end up in the hands of the government has the potential to engender distrust and cost American businesses significant revenues both at home and abroad.[154]

Implications of *United States v. Jones* on the Third-Party Doctrine

In addition to the doctrinal and practical arguments made against the third-party doctrine, several concurring opinions in the recent GPS tracking case *United States v. Jones* prompt additional questions about its continued application. Some argue that these opinions foreshadow a shift in the Court's thinking about the effect of technology on the government's ability to collect large data sets about American citizens.

In *Jones*, the police attached a GPS tracking device to the underbelly of Jones's car and tracked it 24 hours a day for 28 days without a warrant.[155] Under controlling precedent, a person had no reasonable expectation of privacy when traveling on public streets because he has revealed his movements to the public at large.[156] While it appeared that *Jones* required a strict application of this previous case law, the Court ruled 9-0 against the government, and held that the investigative activity there constituted a Fourth Amendment search. The reason why, however, was far from unanimous.

The majority opinion, written by Justice Scalia, and joined by Chief Justice Roberts and Justices Kennedy, Thomas, and Sotomayor, held that the physical attachment of the tracking device on Jones's car, coupled with the intent to obtain information about his movements, amounted to a Fourth Amendment search.[157] When the police attached the device, they physically trespassed onto his vehicle, his "effect," a constitutionally protected area under the Fourth Amendment's protection of "persons, houses, papers, and effects."[158] As Justice Scalia's opinion relied upon a

---

[152] *White*, 401 U.S. at 787 (Harlan, J., dissenting).

[153] *Id.*

[154] *See* John Naughton, *Edward Snowden's Not the Story, the Internet Is*, THE GUARDIAN (July 23, 2013), *available at* http://www.theguardian.com/technology/2013/jul/28/edward-snowden-death-of-internet; Allan Holmes, *NSA Spying Disclosures Could Cost Companies Billions* (Sept. 10, 2013), *available at* http://www.salon.com/2013/09/10/ nsa_spying_disclosures_could_cost_companies_billions_in_sales_newscred/.

[155] United States v. Jones, 132 S. Ct. 945, 948 (2012). The D.C. Metropolitan police had obtained a warrant, but it had expired the day before the device was installed and was installed in the wrong jurisdiction. *Id.* at n.1.

[156] United States v. Knotts, 460 U.S. 276, 281 (1983).

[157] *Jones*, 132 S. Ct. at 949.

[158] *Id.* at 949; U.S. CONST. amend. IV.

trespass theory of the Fourth Amendment, it will likely not have major repercussions for the third-party doctrine, unless one accepts that the government trespasses on an individual's "papers" or "effects" when it accesses records from third-party companies.[159]

However, two concurring opinions in *Jones* by Justices Sotomayor and Alito might signal the willingness of five Justices to reevaluate future applications of the third-party doctrine, at least with respect to pervasive government monitoring. Justice Sotomayor's solo concurrence provided the more far-reaching of the two opinions. She directly called into question "the premise that an individual has no reasonable expectation of privacy in information voluntarily disclosed to third parties."[160] She observed:

> This approach is ill suited to the digital age, in which people reveal a great deal of information about themselves to third parties in the course of carrying out mundane tasks. People disclose the phone numbers that they dial or text to their cellular providers; the URLs that they visit and the e-mail addresses with which they correspond to their Internet service providers; and the books, groceries, and medications they purchase to online retailers.... I for one doubt that people would accept without complaint the warrantless disclosure to the Government of a list of every Web site they had visited in the last week, or month, or year. But whatever the societal expectations, they can attain constitutionally protected status only if our Fourth Amendment jurisprudence ceases to treat secrecy as a prerequisite for privacy. I would not assume that all information voluntarily disclosed to some member of the public for a limited purpose is, for that reason alone, disentitled to Fourth Amendment protection.[161]

It seems that Justice Sotomayor, if not prepared to discard the third-party doctrine in whole, is willing to significantly limit its reach, especially when the government is accessing a wealth of data about an individual. Again, it should be noted that Justice Sotomayor was the only member to articulate this more expansive roll-back of the third-party doctrine.

More generally, both Justices Sotomayor and Alito's opinions could be interpreted to call into question the continued application of the third-party doctrine insofar as it permits pervasive government monitoring. In his concurrence, Justice Alito, joined by Justices Ginsburg, Breyer, and Kagan, found that while short-term monitoring may be permissible under past precedent, "the use of longer term GPS monitoring in investigations of most offenses impinges on expectations of privacy."[162] Justice Sotomayor, who joined the majority but also concurred separately, agreed

---

[159] *See* Smith, *supra* note 15, at 571 ("One possibility is that Scalia's physical trespass analysis applies to digital trespass. After all, if an agent were to digitally connect with your computer, GPS device, or mobile phone for investigatory purposes, she is appropriating your property for purposes of gathering evidence, just like the agents who placed the tracker on your car."); Jack Wade Nowlin, *The Warren Court's House Built on Sand: From Security in Persons, Houses, Papers, and Effects to Mere Reasonableness in Fourth Amendment Doctrine*, 81 MISS. L. J. 1017, 1046-47 (2012) ("On the 'protected interest' view, one would retain one's right to security in the papers against governmental intrusion. The essence of the traditional security in protected interests, grounded in the law of property, is the right to exclude—which, of course, includes the right to selectively include some individuals while excluding others. On this view, one has a right to allow some actors access to one's home or papers while still excluding others—such as the police. It would thus invade the core of the protected interest for the government to obtain papers through a third party and search through them—without the owner's permission.").

[160] *Jones*, 132 S. Ct. at 957 (Sotomayor, J., concurring).

[161] *Id.*

[162] *Jones*, 132 S. Ct. at 964 (Alito, J., concurring).

with Justice Alito's approach and would have gone even further to find that short-term monitoring should be prohibited in some instances.[163]

These five Justices expressed two interrelated concerns. First, they were uneasy about the government's ability to gather, analyze, and use an extensive volume of information about each person's comings and goings. Justice Sotomayor observed that "GPS monitoring generates a precise, comprehensive records of a person's public movements that reflects a wealth of information about her familial, political, professional, religious, and sexual associations."[164] This idea, commonly referred to as the "mosaic theory," posits that the aggregation of information about a person can reveal a whole lot more about him than each part in isolation. The Justices were not the first to espouse this theory. Before the case reached the Supreme Court, the District of Columbia Court of Appeals below articulated a similar sentiment in finding that the government's month-long location tracking constituted a Fourth Amendment search:

> Prolonged surveillance reveals types of information not revealed by short-term surveillance, such as what a person does repeatedly, what he does not do, and what he does ensemble. These types of information can each reveal more about a person than does any individual trip viewed in isolation. Repeated visits to a church, a gym, a bar, or a bookie tell a story not told by any single visit, as does one's not visiting any of these places over the course of a month. The sequence of a person's movements can reveal still more; a single trip to a gynecologist's office tells little about a woman, but that trip followed a few weeks later by a visit to a baby supply store tells a different story. A person who knows all of another's travels can deduce whether he is a weekly church goer, a heavy drinker, a regular at the gym, an unfaithful husband, an outpatient receiving medical treatment, an associate of particular individuals or political groups—and not just one such fact about a person, but all such facts.[165]

In addition to this aggregation issue, the Justices expressed concern about the ability of technology to significantly reduce natural barriers such as limited resources and political accountability that in the past would have limited law enforcement overreach in the field of surveillance.[166] For Justice Alito, the fact that the government simply could not have tracked a person's every movement for a month-long period under traditional law enforcement methods led him to conclude that the tracking was overly intrusive.[167]

While Justice Sotomayor directly criticized the third-party doctrine, one could read Justice Alito's concurrence as limited solely to monitoring conducted directly by government agents, and not extending to instances where third parties collect data on individuals. That being said, the combination of the *Jones* concurrences has already had an effect in third-party cases in lower federal courts. For example, the District Court for the District of Columbia applied a variation of the mosaic theory to invalidate the NSA's collection of telephone call records.[168] Citing to the *Jones* concurrences, Judge Richard H. Leon acknowledged that the type of information collected

---

[163] *Id.* at 957 (Sotomayor, J., concurring).

[164] Jones, 132 S. Ct. at 955.

[165] United States v. Maynard, 615 F.3d 544, 562 (D.C. Cir. 2010).

[166] *See* Jones 132 S. Ct. at 956 (Sotomayor, J., concurring) ("And because GPS monitoring is cheap in comparison to conventional surveillance techniques and, by design, proceeds surreptitiously, it evades the ordinary checks that constrain abusive law enforcement practices: 'limited police resources and community hostility.'") (quoting Illinois v. Lidster, 540 U.S. 419, 426 (2004)).

[167] *Jones*, 132 S. Ct. at 964 (Alito, J., concurring).

[168] Klayman v. Obama, 957 F. Supp. 2d 1, 36 (D.D.C. 2013).

under the NSA's metadata program was very similar to that upheld in *Smith*, "but the ubiquity of phones has dramatically altered the *quantity* of information that is now available and, *more importantly*, what that information can tell the Government about people's lives."[169] And, as described above, judges in certain cell phone location monitoring cases have applied *Jones* and the mosaic theory to deem months-long government tracking a Fourth Amendment search.[170] In the long run, it may take a more pertinent set of facts for the Justices to advance the arguments enunciated in *Jones*.

Congressional Response to the Third-Party Doctrine

Notwithstanding the concurring opinions in *Jones*, the bulk of Supreme Court and lower federal court precedent have left most non-content information unprotected by the Fourth Amendment. In some instances, Congress filled this void by creating varying levels of privacy protection for this type of non-content information. However, these protections are in the main not as robust as the warrant requirement, and in some instances, searches may be justified by little more than "official curiosity."[171]

Seven years after the Court handed down *Smith* and ruled that government access to telephone toll records was not covered by the Fourth Amendment, Congress enacted as part of the Electronic Communications Privacy Act of 1986 (ECPA) several provisions requiring the government to seek a court order before using a pen register or trap and trace device.[172] Again, these devices allow the government to gather dialed telephone numbers and email addressing information, among other non-content information.[173] Under 18 U.S.C. § 3123, a court "shall issue an ex parte order authorizing the installation and use of a pen register or trap and trace device ... if the court finds that the attorney for the Government has certified that the information likely to be obtained by such installation and use is relevant to an ongoing criminal investigation."[174]

A few things should be noted about this provision. First, the "shall" language removes discretion from the judge; if the judge finds the government has made the required certification, he must issue the order.[175] Second, while the court must ensure that the government has made the proper certification, ECPA does not require an "independent judicial inquiry into the veracity of the

---

[169] *Id.* at 35-36.

[170] *In re* Application of the United States of America for an Order Authorizing the Release of Historical Cell-Site Information, 809 F. Supp. 2d 113, 126 (E.D.N.Y. 2011).

[171] *See* United States v. Morton Salt Co., 338 U.S. 632, 652 (1950) (describing relevancy standard for subpoenas).

[172] Electronic Communications Privacy Act of 1986, P.L. 99-508, § 301, 100 Stat 1848.

[173] As enacted in 1986, the pen register statute, by its terms, only authorized the interception of *telephone* metadata. 100 Stat. 1871 ("[T]he term 'pen register' means a device which records or decodes electronic or other impulses which identify the numbers dialed or otherwise transmitted on the *telephone line* to which such device is attached.") (emphasis added). Congress extended the pen register/trap and trace authority to also cover Internet addressing information as part of the United and Strengthening America by Providing Appropriate Tools Required to Intercept and Obstruct Terrorism (USA PATRIOT Act) of 2001, P.L. 107-56, §216, 115 Stat. 272, 288, *codified at* 18 U.S.C. § 3127.

[174] 18 U.S.C. § 3123.

[175] *See* United States v. Fregoso, 60 F.3d 1314, 1320 (8th Cir. 1995) ("The judicial role in approving use of trap and trace devices is ministerial in nature because, upon a proper application being made under 18 U.S.C. § 3122, 'the court shall enter an ex parte order authorizing the installation' of such a device. 18 U.S.C. § 3123(a)") (emphasis in original)).

attested facts."[176] This means that the judge will not make an independent assessment whether the relevancy standard has been met, but only that the government has made the proper certification. One district court has noted that "the extremely limited judicial review required by [the pen register statute] is intended merely to safeguard against purely random use of this device."[177] One magistrate judge went so far as to describe his role under the pen register statute as a "rubber stamp" limited to "proofreading errors," and that "without independent judicial review, the authorization of pen registers is subject to misuse and abuse."[178] Third, the relevancy standard, which again the government, and not the court, determines if it has been met, is a "far from burdensome" legal standard.[179] The Supreme Court has held, at least in the subpoena context, that information sought is not relevant only if "there is no reasonable possibility that the category of materials the Government seeks will produce information relevant to the general subject" of the investigation.[180] In light of this relatively lax standard, several prominent commentators on privacy and technology have suggested that Congress should increase the evidentiary threshold under Section 3123 from mere relevance to at least a reasonable suspicion standard similar to that used for accessing certain stored communications.[181]

Also included in ECPA is the Stored Communications Act (SCA), in which Congress provided varying degrees of protection to information historically subject to the third-party doctrine and, thus, outside the reach of the Fourth Amendment. Under 18 U.S.C. § 2703(c), service providers must hand over "records or other information pertaining to a subscriber" so long as the government can establish "specific and articulable facts" that the records are "relevant and material" to an ongoing criminal investigation.[182] This is akin to the *Terry* reasonable suspicion standard—it is lower than probable cause but does require the government to articulate its basis to believe that the information is connected to criminal activity.[183] This standard has been applied to data such as the to/from address line in an email or the IP addresses of websites a person has visited. Some courts have construed Section 2703(d) in conjunction with the pen register statute to allow the government access to cell site location information.[184] Section 2703(c)(2) requires the providers to hand over other customer information such as their name, address, telephone calling records, length of service, telephone number, and means and source of payments,

[176] *In re* Application of the United States of America for an Order Authorizing the Installation and Use of a Pen Register and Trap and Trace Device, 846 F. Supp. 1555, 1559 (M.D. Fla. 1994); *see also* S. Rpt. 99-541, at 47 (1986) ("[Section 3123] does not envision an independent judicial review of whether the application meets the relevance standard, rather the court needs only to review the completeness of the certification submitted.").

[177] United States v. Hallmark, 911 F.2d 399, 402 (10th 1990).

[178] *In re* Application of the United States of America for an Order Authorizing the Installation and Use of a Pen Register and Trap and Trace Device, 846 F. Supp. 1555, 1564-65, 1563 n.4 (M.D. Fla. 1994).

[179] *In Re* of Applications of the United States of America for Orders (1) Authorizing the Use of Pen Registers and Trap and Trace Devices and (2) Authorizing Release of Subscriber Information, 515 F. Supp. 2d 325, 329 (E.D.N.Y. 2007).

[180] United States v. R. Enterprises, Inc., 498 U.S. 292, 301 (1991).

[181] *See Anti-Terrorism Investigations and the Fourth Amendment After September 11, 2001: Hearing Before the Subcomm. on the Constitution of the H. Comm. of the Judiciary*, 108th Cong. 21, 26 (2003) (statements of James Dempsey, Center for Democracy and Technology, and Orin S. Kerr, Law Professor).

[182] 18 U.S.C. § 2703(d).

[183] *In re* Application of the United States of America for an Order Pursuant to 18 U.S.C. § 2703(d), 707 F.3d 283, 287 (4th Cir. 2013).

[184] *In re* Application of the United States of America for an Order for Disclosure of Telecommunications Records and Authorizing the Use of a Pen Register and Trap and Trace, 405 F. Supp. 2d 435, 449-50 (S.D.N.Y. 2005).

including credit card or bank account numbers with either an administrative, grand jury, or trial subpoena.[185]

Additionally, Congress has passed more targeted privacy protection laws. For instance, the privacy of cable subscribers is safeguarded under the Cable Communications Privacy Act of 1984,[186] and the privacy of video store customers under the Video Privacy Protection Act.[187]

More recently, various Members of Congress have sought to temper the reach of the third-party doctrine with respect to transactional data. Several days after the Edward Snowden leaks became public, Senator Paul filed the "Fourth Amendment Restoration Act of 2013" (S. 1121) in an effort to "stop the National Security Agency from spying on citizens of the United States[.]"[188] This bill would require that "[t]he Fourth Amendment to the Constitution shall not be construed to allow any agency of the United States Government to search the phone records of Americans without a warrant based upon probable cause."[189] While dictating to the judiciary what the Fourth Amendment should and should not protect may be beyond Congress's constitutional power,[190] Congress clearly can play a role in setting substantive and procedural limitations on government surveillance authorities. For instance, Senator Paul has introduced a similar bill, the "Fourth Amendment Preservation and Protection Act of 2013" (S. 1037), which would prohibit federal, state, and local government officials from accessing information relating to an individual held by a third party in a "system of records."[191] Other congressional measures would alter the third-party doctrine in a more targeted way. Several location monitoring bills would, for instance, prohibit companies from sharing their customers' location information unless the government obtained a warrant or one of several limited exceptions applied.[192]

Conclusion

So what does the future have in store for the third-party doctrine and the government's collection of non-content, transactional data? At this point, there appears to be only one solid vote on the Court in Justice Sotomayor for eliminating or significantly reducing the scope of this doctrine. Although there are hints in Justice Alito's *Jones* opinion that he and the three members of his concurrence are ready to reconsider this rule when it comes to pervasive government surveillance, his rationale was left somewhat underdeveloped. It will take future opinions to get a better sense of whether or how far these Justices are willing to go to limit government access to non-content information held in the hands of third parties. In the meantime, the lower federal courts might continue to limit or distinguish the third-party doctrine in specific and narrow instances. For instance, in the NSA telephone metadata case, Judge Leon limited *Smith* to its facts and held that

---

[185] 18 U.S.C. § 2703(c)(2).

[186] 47 U.S.C. § 551; *see* Kerr, *supra* note 123, at 855 ("A broader look at the legal standards that govern criminal investigations involving new technologies suggests that Congress has often taken the lead, and that judicial decisions interpreting the Fourth Amendment generally have played a secondary role").

[187] 18 U.S.C. § 2710.

[188] Fourth Amendment Restoration Act of 2013, S. 1121 (1st Sess. 2013).

[189] *Id.*

[190] *See* Dickerson v. United States, 530 U.S. 428, 437 (2000) ("Congress may not legislatively supersede our decisions interpreting and applying the Constitution.").

[191] Fourth Amendment Preservation and Protection Act of 2013, S. 1037, 113th Cong. (1st Sess. 2013).

[192] *See, e.g.*, Geolocation Privacy and Surveillance Act, S. 639, H.R. 1312, 113th Cong (1st Sess. 2013).

it did not apply to this more comprehensive data collection program.[193] Likewise, if and when the Supreme Court is asked to reconsider the scope of the third-party doctrine, it is more likely to carve out specific exceptions than to overturn it in its entirety. This approach would permit the courts to engage in a more nuanced, normative approach to analyzing the privacy interests implicated by accessing records derived from transactions between people and other various entities.

Another possibility is for Congress to act. Justice Alito observed in *Jones* that "[i]in circumstances involving dramatic technological change, the best solution to privacy concerns may be legislative" as "a legislative body is well situated to gauge changing public attitudes, to draw detailed lines, and to balance privacy and public safety in a comprehensive way."[194] This argument that Congress is best suited to address the nuanced policy questions that privacy and security entails has been expressed by commentators as well.[195] Like the courts, it appears unlikely that Congress would be willing to completely eliminate the third-party doctrine. On the other hand, Congress may be more inclined to engage in a subject-by-subject approach, in which Congress limits the third-party doctrine in certain areas. Congress provided statutory protection for telephone toll records in the pen register/trap and trace statute; for Internet metadata in the Stored Communications Act; and for video customer records in the Video Privacy Protection Act. It could enact similar protection for other subject areas where non-content information is shared with companies as a necessary part of doing business.

Author Contact Information

Richard M. Thompson II
Legislative Attorney
rthompson@crs.loc.gov, 7-8449

---

[193] *Klayman*, 957 F. Supp. 2d at 37 ("[T]he *Smith* pen register and the ongoing NSA Bulk Telephony Metadata Program have so many significant distinctions between them that I cannot possibly navigate these uncharted Fourth Amendment waters using as my North Star a case that predates the rise of cell phones.").

[194] *Jones*, 132 S. Ct. at 964.

[195] Kerr, *supra* note 123, at 857.